Learn Hangul in One Hour!

A Complete Course on How to Teach Yourself the Korean Writing System

By Allen Williams PhD

ACKNOWLEDGEMENTS

This little book would not have been possible without the help of many contributors. Those include the students of Korean and my friends who have encouraged me to find a better, easier way to learn and remember the Korean writing system. A special thanks to my friend Dr. Namwon Heo for his help in choosing the example words and vocabulary for this book. And to my good friend Dr. Hyocheol Kim for his diligence, persistence, and hard work in preparing the diagrams that appear in this book.

Thank you to Jeff Carneal, for believing in me and my ideas, and for giving me 'llama' for the mnemonic sentences for remembering the dictionary order.

Thanks as well to my friends, Pongsu, Austin, Will, Joseph, Joe, and the rest for the feedback and providing the guinea pigs for testing the drafts of this book.

Thanks to my wife who has made nagging into a fine art of encouragement and motivation. Without your patience, love, and support none of this would have reached fruition.

And, thanks to you the readers for studying Korean. Good luck with your study. I hope this little book helps.

Although I have tried to make it as error free as possible, you may find something. I take full responsibility for any mistakes you may find.

If you have comments, suggestions, or questions, please visit www.LearnKoreanFast.com and contact me via the contact information there. I would love to hear from you and be happy to help you in any way that I can.

CONTENTS

INTRODUCTION

This book is intended to teach you to learn and remember the Korean writing alphabet. This alphabet is called Hangul, and has been heralded by some to be one of the most scientific writing systems in use today. However, since it varies greatly from the English alphabet, it can appear daunting at first and traditional methods for learning and remembering it are boring and time consuming. If you follow the steps set forth in this book, you will accomplish this task, and you will do it in only 1 hour. 1 hour of concentrated study on the ideas set forth in this book.

I am not a Korean language teacher in the formal sense, but I have spent a good deal of time studying the Korean language as well as a smattering of time on a couple of other languages. I wrote this book in response to the frustrations I've seen from those who were struggling to learn Korean but were doing it by following romanized versions of the words. I hate to see time and talent wasted, and to me, that is just what that kind of study is, a waste. If you're in Korea, you will see very little romanization (or other English spelling representations). Outside of road signs and a few restaurant menus, Hangul is the prevalent method for writing Korean, and it is well worth the time it takes to learn and remember it. Also, once you have mastered the alphabet, you will be surprised at how many things you are able to understand, especially since there are a great deal of foreign words in use in Korea but represented in Hangul and with a slightly different pronunciation. If you truly want to learn Korean, then learning Hangul is the first and most sensible step.

This book will teach you to do this, learning on your own or in a group. Chinese characters are also used to represent the Korean language, but it is becoming less and less used though it still appears in newspaper headlines and many Koreans' name or business cards. This book won't be dealing with those characters. You will also need to continue your usage of your new found knowledge in order to permanently ingrain it into your memory and apply this knowledge to acquiring vocabulary. I am sure you will find this book helpful in starting you on the path to a wonderful experience with your study of Korean or stay in Korea.

HOW TO USE THIS BOOK
(Don't skip this part!!)

The characters and lessons have been arranged in a manner as to make them the easiest to learn and will be grouped accordingly. You will find a chart at the end of this book that will show you the basic dictionary order along with a page number for reference. One deviation from that order has been the inclusion of the 'double letters' and vowels. I will explain more about this later.

As we make key words for remembering letters in English, for example A is for Apple, choose one of the example words given after the introduction of each character and use it for your reference point for pronunciation. After each lesson, take a break. Ideally you should take at least 2 to 3 days to finish the exercises rather than trying to burn your way through in one sitting. There is no real difference in difficulty level from lesson to lesson though you might have to take a bit of time at first to adopt and adapt to the method. There are 39 different characters and combinations, and they are divided in to three lessons containing 13 characters each. You should need about 20 minutes to complete each lesson, hence the one hour of study time. The break time is essential to assimilating the information so don't skip it. Studies also show that our brains tend to remember the first and last parts of information the easiest so it makes sense for us to create as many 'firsts' and 'lasts' to take advantage of our brain's natural tendencies.

At the top of each page you will see the character followed by the explanation and the keys to remembering it, the pronunciation, and a few short, simple words to be used for practice and testing your knowledge. You will also see diagrams that show first the way the characters look when typed, an example of a hand printed style, and where it is necessary an example of a more cursive writing style. In the example sections I've tried to provide as many useful words as possible. This way you can also pick up some vocabulary as you go. But don't spend too much time trying to remember the words. They are mainly for you to use for reading practice. You can always come back to them later to review their meanings. Before moving on to the next lesson, be sure that you've made the images as big, bright, silly, and as memorable as you can.

Take a moment now to open this book to any page

displaying a character and familiarize yourself with the layout.

At the end of the lessons I have included a few things you might find helpful in using this book as a reference later and in continuing your Korean language study. You will also find a section on how to remember the dictionary order of Hangul. You will be able to apply this method and remember easily and quickly in about the time it takes you to read the text. I have also included some study tips that I have used for acquiring vocabulary and practicing pronunciation. These are general principles that can be applied to learning any language.

Let me clear up a couple of things before we begin. First, Korean doesn't have exact matches in standard English for many of the characters. I have tried to use the closest approximations, but you should follow this up with practice with a native speaker if possible to make sure you are getting the pronunciation correct. Also, since phonetics and romanization tend to differ and not everyone who comes into contact with this book knows the International Phonetic Alphabet by heart, I've tried to make it as easy as possible by just using words and letter groupings that will convey the idea without sending you to a dictionary or pronunciation guide. The purpose of this book is to teach you to read, write, and remember the Hangul characters and not to make you learn a lot of technical language and special vocabulary usually reserved for linguists. Also, if you've already learned a few characters, don't be tempted to try to shortcut the process. I urge you to follow the guidelines set out in the book as one example is often built from another's explanation. At the end of each lesson you will find a box for writing down the time it took you to complete it. Each lesson should take about 20 minutes.

While it's likely that no one book can cover everything, and certainly not one as short as this, a good thing about Hangul is that it is a fairly consistent writing and sounding system. And this book will cover fairly thoroughly the basic and usual pronunciations of the Korean characters. There are a few exceptions where certain characters when appearing together have a pronunciation that differs from their usual. We won't be going into that here since it is probably best to deal with those when you meet them. The good thing is there are really very few of those exceptions and those exceptions remain very consistent.

Lesson One

Before you begin, make sure that you've read through the introduction of this book and especially the section marked "How to Use This Book." When you are ready to begin, write down the time you start in the box below and go to the next page. Remember that learning should be fun! Ready? Then let's get started!

Start Time	

이

No Korean character can stand on its own. It appears in either a consonant-vowel or consonant-vowel-consonant pattern. So let's take first things first and introduce a very useful character iŭng, ㅇ. Its sound is the 'ng' sound, and since it looks like a 'ring' we can get that in our memory very easily. However, if it appears first in the spelling, it remains silent and acts as a place holder as it does now in the vowel 이.

Our vowels are mainly built on a stick ㅣ. It looks like an 'i' and we can give it the phonetic pronunciation of 'ee'. Simple as that we have our first vowel and the foundation for many more.

Since we don't have much to work with yet here, we'll need to wait for some example words, but a good one for us to start with is 이 itself which means 'two.'

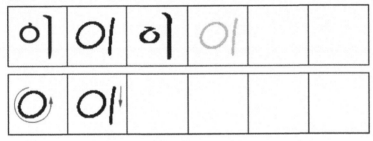

$\underline{\overset{\text{o}}{\text{o}}}$

We have our stick for the vowels here and it's pointing straight across. If the stick is on your tongue, then your tongue is laying flat in your mouth and you are just pushing the sound out. Remember to keep your lips straight across, too and you'll have a fair representation of the $\underline{\text{o}}$ sound of u. There's really no exact pronunciation for this in English as it falls a little between the u of 'put' and oo of 'boot.'

Example words:
No example words yet.

의

This is a simple diphthong formed by combining —
and ㅣ. If you pronounce these in succession you'll
have the 'ui' sound of the vowel 의. In this form (의)
it most often appears at the end of nouns to show
possession like the 's (ie John's) in English.

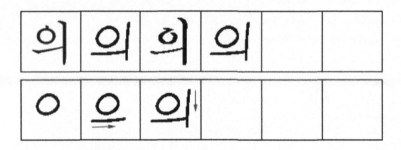

Example words:
No example words possible yet.

아

Our next vowel is 'ah' represented by 아. We have our stick from before with a short protrusion. Pretend it's your tongue. Then just stick out your tongue and say 'ah'. Remember we have to have our ㅇ as a place holder and you've got it.

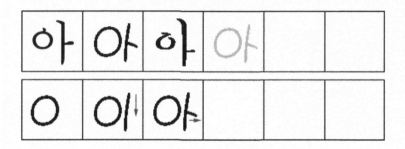

Example words:
아 : oh
아이 : toddler

અ

If you could suck your tongue backwards, you'd probably make the sound you would if someone hit you a little too hard in the pit of the stomach, 'uh.' (This only works in theory. Don't try this!!!) Take a moment to make sure you've got the sound and direction of the 'tongue' down then review our આ sound to make sure.

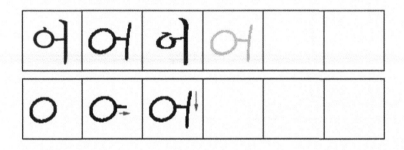

Example words:
No example words possible yet.

애

We have here a vowel that looks a little like an A (pronounced as a long 'a.') that's been pried apart at the top. And that's what the sound is, and it is formed by combining ㅏ with ㅣ. If you're more comfortable with the representation of the letter H, try this. If you pronounce the letter H very slowly, as if it had two syllables, what's the first sound? Ay-ch!

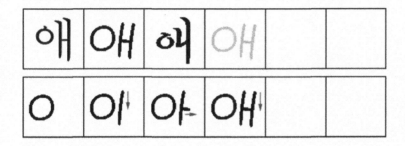

Example words:
애 : child

에

This vowel is a combination of ㅓ and ㅣ. But the pronunciation is still very similar to that of a long 'a' sound in English. Although it originally was pronounced more like 'eh,' the difference is almost indistinguishable from Koreans under 40 years of age.

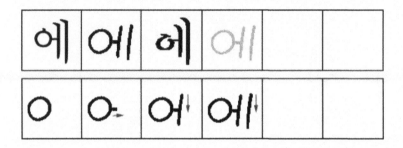

Example words:
-에 : to (something or place)

ㄴ

At first you might not think our niŭn, ㄴ, resembles a nose, at least not yours, but on closer look we see it's not an ordinary nose, but a nose it is. Perhaps it's the now flat nose of a club fighter that went too many rounds. There you have it: nose, niŭn, and the n sound.

Example words:

나 : me
나이 : age
나의 : my

마

My oh my! It's a square mouth! Most of us know the first sound that makes sense that comes from our mouth as a baby is 'mama' because it's one of the most natural sounds for our mouths to form. That makes it only sensible that miŭm, ㅁ, gives us the first mouth sound of m.

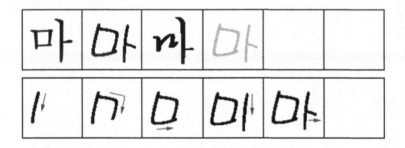

Example words:
만 : 10,000
매너 : manner
마음 : mind

하

Here's one that's a little different from the others. ㅎ is hiŭt, and gives us the h sound. Picture this as the head and hat of a happy, hopping snowman and you should get the h sound implanted into your own head.

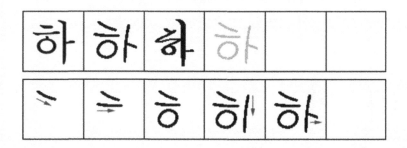

Example words:

하마 : hippo

힘 : strength

하나 : one

파

Let's pretend we want to make a little pen to hold in something, like a pig pen. When you build a pen you usually start from the ground up, but remember our writing rules that the top lines come first. Look at the writing example. It even looks a little like the bars on a prison window, doesn't it? Now we have the p sound of p'iŭp, ㅍ.

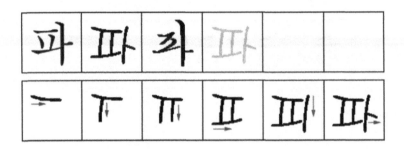

Example words:
피 : blood
파마 : a permanent (for hair)
피아노 : piano

오

Here we have our 'ring' ○ above ㅗ. Picture the ring toss at the carnival, and you are tossing letter O's at the peg. Oh! so close! But you should be able to remember that 오 is the 'oh' sound in Korean.

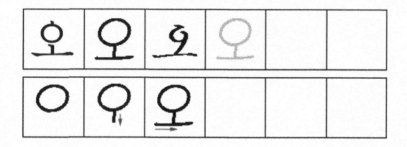

Example words:
오 : five
오이 : cucumber
노인 : elderly person

우

Let's stay with our ring toss image of 오, but this time just as the ring approaches the peg turns downward 우 and Ooops! You missed again. You didn't miss the pronunciation clue though, did you? That's right. It's the *oo* sound of 'boo' represented in Korean by 우.

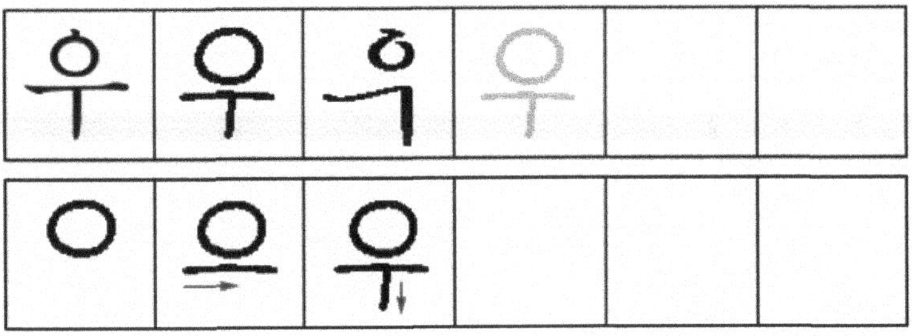

우	우	우	우		
ㅇ	오	우			

Example words:
우아 : elegant
문 : door
오후 : afternoon

Since we weren't able to make a lot of example words with our first few characters, here are a few to give you some reading practice and test your memory. These don't include all of the characters we've met in this unit, but do include the characters who previously didn't have example words.

Example words for Lesson One:

나의 : my   흠모 : admiration
해 : sun   희망 : hope
펜 : pen   메모 : memo
엄마 : mom   매우 : very

And that's the end of Lesson One! Check the time and write it in the box below.

Finish	
Total	

Now take a break from your study. When you are ready to begin again . . .

Go to Lesson Two.

Lesson Two

If you came straight here without a break, stop now. I know you don't feel tired and you're having fun, but your brain needs some time to assimilate the information we just gave it so take some time now to get a breather and let your brain do its work while you are thinking about something else. If you did take your break and want to get started again, take just a moment to recap the last section and make sure you've got those characters firmly in your mind. Review by scanning the example words of Lesson One. Don't spend a lot of time on the meanings, just make sure you can read them aloud.

Now are you ready to get back to the fun? Check the clock and write your time in the box below and you'll be on your way with Lesson Two.

Start Time	

가

This is as easy to write as it is to remember. We just start to write a capital G from the bottom upwards. G Try it a few times below and see how easy it sticks in your mind. This gives us the 'g' sound in the initial position and a harder almost 'k' sound in the final position. It's name is giyŏk and now we can go, go, go on to other things.

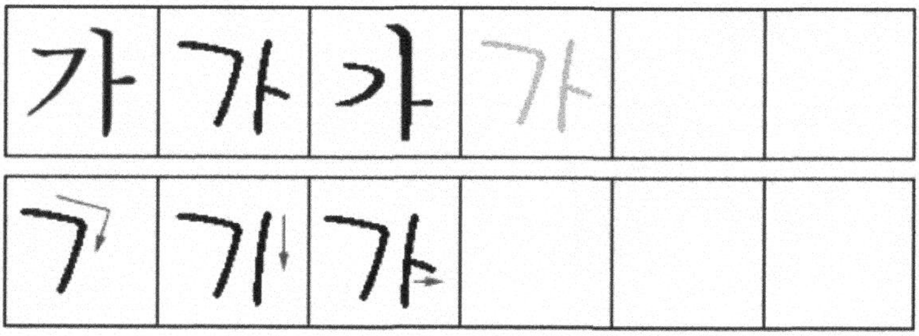

가	가	가	가		
ㄱ	가	가			

Example words:
아기: baby
강 : river
학 : crane (the bird)

까

Chalk this one up as already learned as we meet the first of five Korean characters that are formed by doubling other characters. Since we already have the ㄱ firmly implanted in our memory, the double giyŏk, ㄲ, is no problem. The sound is longer and moved a bit more towards the back of the throat.

Example words:
아까 : just before
꿈 : dream
꼬끼오 : cock-a-doodle-doo

카

Now we need to add an easy stroke that's sort of a radical. The short stroke (-) is like an air valve. It usually appears on top of a character but sometimes is inside. It's not so difficult to spot and simply means to aspirate the pronunciation of the character it appears with. Here you see our air valve inside of a slightly larger ㄱ. This gives us the k sound of k'iŭk, ㅋ.

Example words:

카 : car

키 : height

코 : nose

다

Just like ㄱ is only a part of the letter whose sound it represents, digŭt, ㄷ, is the front part of the letter d. Keep in mind that almost all Korean letters are made up of lines. Horizontal lines go from left to right, and vertical lines go from top to bottom. That means that instead of a round shape for the front of our d, we get ㅁ that forms ㄷ. And that gives us our d sound.

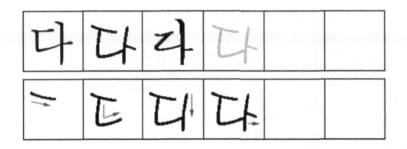

Example words:
다 : all
가다 : to go
등등 : etc. etc.

따

The second of our double characters is the double digŭt. This one is probably most closely approximated by the voiced 'th' sound as in 'that.' Be careful to limit the aspiration and exhaling of air as pronounce it though and keep it short.

Example words:

때 : grime

땀 : sweat

떠나다 : to leave

타

As you probably know (if you don't, no problem, now you do!), the English *d* and *t* are formed in the same way with the lips, teeth and tongue with the only difference being the *t* is pronounced with air (aspirated) and the *d* is voiced. So we take our ㄷ for the *d* sound and place our air valve inside: ㄷ + ㅡ to get ㅌ, tiŭt.

Example words:
타다 : to ride
낙타 : camel
통 : container

라

This one is a *real* dandy. It's the most presumptuous character of our group since it's actually made up of a small ㄱ placed on top of a ㄷ to form ㄹ. The name gives us our sound and to get that you need only imagine you're from West Tennessee where no true one syllable words exist. Stretch out the pronunciation of 'real' to 'ree–uhl' and you've got the name and starting sound for riŭl, ㄹ. This character has the *r* sound in initial position but sounds a little more like *L* in the final position.

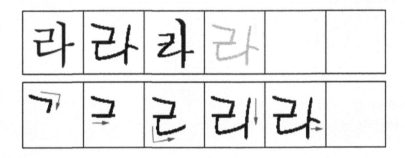

Example words:
나라 : country
라디오 : radio

야

This time we have the 아 and an extra tongue. Yuck! The vowels with two marks are used to add a *y* pronunciation, so 아 simply becomes 야, or 'yah.' Lucky for us there are several of these vowels that you can form by adding the extra tongue and placing the *y* sound in front. Simple, isn't it?

Example words:
야간 : night (as an adjective: night class)
약 : medicine
뺨 : cheek

여

Follow that up with another freebie. Just add the *y* to our 어 sound and you have the pronunciation of 여, 'yuh.' Easier than you thought? Starting to think learning doesn't have to be hard, or boring? Hope so.

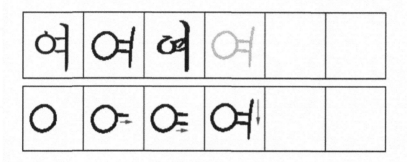

Example words:

역 : station

여우 : fox

여행 : travel

요

Just add the *y* to 오 and you've now got *yo*, 요. Too easy? Admit it. It's easier than you thought and fun, isn't it?

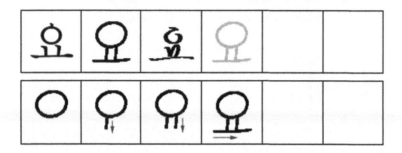

Example words:

요요 : yoyo

요금 : fare

학교 : school

I'm sure you never thought it would be this easy, but it is. Here's another 'give me'. Just take our 우 sound and add *y* to get the *yoo* of 유. A great word to pair these up and plant them permanently in your memory is 우유, which means 'milk.'

유	유	유	유		
ㅇ	오	오	오		

Example words:

우유 : milk
유아 : infant
유리 : glass

애

Another 'double tongue' sound formed by adding ㅑ to
ㅣ. Since we know that if there are two lines we only
need to add *y* to get the proper pronunciation, we now
have the *ye* (or maybe *yay* is easier?) sound.

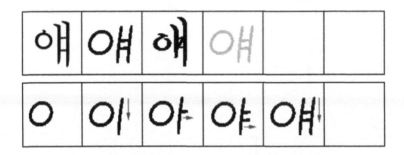

Example words:
No example words possible yet.

예

This is the pair sound for our previous compound vowel so we need only remember what we learned from before. Modern Koreans make no distinction when speaking either 예 or 애.

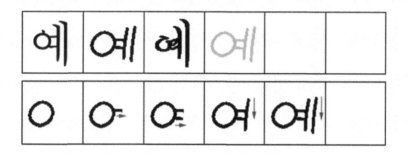

Example words:

예 : yes

계란 : egg

예약 : reservation

Time for another break and now you're more than half finished!! Make sure that you take at least a 10 minute break. Walk around, get something to drink and clear your mind before moving on to the next lesson. Be sure to write your time for this lesson in the box below.

Finish Lesson 2	
Total	

Lesson Three

Are you ready to start the last lesson? If you didn't take a break, be sure to do that before you continue. You should be feeling pretty confident by now and be able to move through the exercises a little more quickly, but not too quickly. Take the time to make each image and character clear before tackling the next. Write down the time and then . . .

Start Time	

자

Here we get the first deviation from our straight up and down or across only lines. We have a 7 with a short stick *J*ammed under it to hold it up. This gives us the *j* sound of jiŭt, ㅈ. Play the image through a few times in your mind until it sticks.

Example words:
자 : ruler (for measuring)
자유 : free (as in free time)
자다 : to sleep

짜

Add to our list the double ㅈ, ㅉ. It's a fun one to say, but the tendency is to get too much of a 'ch' sound so stay on the 'j' sound. It is pronounced a little longer and more forcefully than the single one. The tongue gets a good vibration going and the air explodes out of the mouth. Have fun with it and exaggerate the pronunciation until it feels right.

Example words:
짜다 : salty
찌르다 : to poke
짜증 : annoyance

차

Take a close look here and you will see our 'air valve' on top of a ㅈ. So, 자, ja becomes 차, cha. And that gives us the sound for ch'iŭt, ㅊ. This stroke sometimes appears across the top of the character, but it can also be in a vertical position as you will see in the writing samples below. It's still easy to spot so don't sweat it.

Example words:
차 : tea
자동차 : automobile
가르치다 : to teach

바

It just gets easier and easier. This letter closely resembles its sound, the letter b. We can only use straight lines though going either across, up, or down. So we have ㅂ and BAM!! *Better* than *Batman Bopping* the *Bad Boys* you have the b sounding biŭp committed to memory. It tends to be a bit softer in the initial position and stronger and closer to a very soft p in the final position.

Example words:
버터 : butter
대답하다 : to answer
밥 : rice

빠

Yes, easier and easier as we slide another double character under our belt with the double biŭp, ㅃ. The best way to pronounce this is like the other doubles, making the sound longer and more explosive.

Example words:
빨리 : fast, quickly
뼈 : a bone
뽀뽀 : light kiss

사

This time we have two short sticks stacked at a steep slope. Surely you see it's the s sound by now. Need more? Can you see a slithering snake snapped in the center? That gives us the siot, ㅅ. When it appears with the ㅣ though it has a slight 'sh' sound.

Example words:
산 : mountain
사다 : to buy
사랑 : love

싸

As we come to this double character let's learn the name for these kinds of twins. These are called 쌍 characters. And this word in Korean is kind enough to use this character in its spelling. It's just the s sound made a bit longer. This time however when it appears with the vowel ㅣ it doesn't have the 'sh' sound.

Example words:
싹 : (noun) sprout, bud
비싼 : expensive
쌍꺼풀 : double eyelid

외

Here's a 'w' vowel that acts a little differently. We have our initial ㅗ vowel so we know it starts with the 'w' sound, but it isn't 'w' + ㅣ. This compound vowel forms the 'way' sound. The best way to remember it is by the meaning of this particular combination. 외 means 'outside.' If you think of this as 'way out' you'll have the sound and the meaning all in one shot.

Example words:
외국 : foreign country
회사 : company
괴롭다 : troublesome

위

A simple compound that gives us another 'w' vowel plus the last vowel of ㅣ and sounds like 'we' as in 'We did it!'

Example words:
위험 : danger
위대한 : great
가위 : scissors

웨

Here we have a compounded compound vowel that at first glance looks a bit convoluted, but on a closer look we see we have just a 'W' added to the 'eh' sound to get a sound that most closely resembles the 'we' sound in *wedding.*

Example words:

웨딩 : wedding

웬일 : what matter, what cause

뒈지다 : kick the bucket

왜

Here we have a compound vowel formed with another compound vowel. Wow! Sounds complicated, but it isn't. We have ㅗ with ㅐ. Just remember our rule about compound vowels that begin with either ㅗ or 우 and add 'w' to the last vowel. Presto! You have the 'way' sound. Don't push too hard into that 'y' at the end. It's only here now for you to know that the 'a' is long. Be sure to say this aloud to get the feel and the correct sound.

Example words:
왜 : why
괘씸하다 : to be insolent
괜히 : in vain

와

Here's an interesting combo of ㅗ and ㅏ. If you pronounce these together, 'oh' + 'ah', the sound of this compound vowel is found in the middle as 'wah'. Try this aloud a couple of times and you'll get it right away. This gives us another rule we can carry in to the other compound vowels. If there is an ㅗ or ㅜ in the initial position of the compound vowel, we just add 'w' to the final vowel sound.

Example words:
과자 : snack
과일 : fruit
화장품 : cosmetics

워

Here's another compound vowel and one of the most common ones. We have the ㅜ in front of ㅓ so just have to remember to put 'w' + ㅓ and we get the 'wuh' sound.

Example words:
공원 : park
원 : Korean currency
식권 : meal ticket

And that's it! Congratulations! You're finished. Just like that you've got the 40 (remember that ㅇ?) different letters of the Korean alphabet. Be sure to check your start time and write the time taken for this section in the box below. Then add them up and put the total time in the box provided.

For a refresher, wait a day or two and then just read through this book in the order of the lessons. Then turn to the back pages to the index of vocabulary. Just read through the list there. If you find there are characters you don't remember, go back to it in the book and re-read the explanation and try to get the image more clearly and firmly implanted in your mind. I'm sure you won't find many of these, but don't worry. Just review the material until you can recognize the characters at a glance.

Lesson 2 Total	
Lesson 1 Total	
Total Time	

Finish Lesson 3	
Total	

POSTSCRIPT

You did it! The important thing now is for you to use your new skill, immediately. If you're in Korea, opportunities abound. My favorite trick was to try to read the signs on every building I passed while riding on a bus or in a taxi. While seated or stopped anywhere, look around you and try to read as much of what you see as you can. Don't worry about not understanding what you are reading at first. That part will come in time if you continue your study. You can also just flip back through this book and read through the example words. At the end of this book you will find some more words in 한글 for you to practice your reading skills and begin to build some vocabulary. I've chosen a group of mostly foreign words in use in Korean to help you learn them more quickly and get some understanding of how those words differ in sound from their English originals.

Some other tips even if you're not in Korea: If you doodle while you're on the phone, doodle in 한글. Write the person's name you are talking with, write English words in 한글, write your own name, try to spell out the objects you see around you, etc. What you are writing then is not as important as the act of writing.

As you continue to write, be sure to watch that the strokes are in the correct order and direction. If you are having problems getting your writing to look right, ask someone who has good Korean writing skill to see if they can point out some things to make your writing better. Knowing the ways the characters are formed and from writing the characters yourself, you will also now be much more able to recognize handwritten Korean which can vary greatly (as does English) when written in a more cursive style. You may find that you are like me and your Korean writing is decidedly easier to read than your English!

Unless you are doing this for someone who does not know how to read Korean, never ever write another Korean word in anything but 한글. I can't stress the importance of this enough. It may save you some time at that moment, but in the long run, the time saved will not amount to the ability lost from not using your skill and ability to write in 한글.

In the following pages you will find indexes for the characters, one in the order they appear in the lessons in this book and the other in their complete dictionary order. I have included the vowels as they would appear after the vowell 아. I have yet to see a list like this in any of the dictionaries or Korean textbooks I have used. It can be very frustrating to the beginner and even the more experienced to find words in a dictionary that contain those compound vowels since they are not usually listed. I also inserted the double characters although they appear after the character they are doubling and without their own headings.

A NOTE ON THE DICTIONARY ORDER OF 한글.

The vowels always appear after the consonants in the dictionary. That is you will first see 가, then words that begin with 가, 거, 겨, and so on through the compound vowels that are applicable. This is then followed by all the words that begin with 나 for ㄴ and then 냐, 너, 녀 as with ㄱ. The 쌍 characters usually appear at the end of the section for the letter it doubles (ie. ㄲ follows ㄱ, ㅆ follows ㅅ etc.) but some dictionaries insert them into the vowel sequence as they appear there. It will take some time to get used to that order, but knowing the sequence will make it easier and faster for you to find words in a Korean/English dictionary. Also, using a dictionary often will help to reinforce the order for you.

HOW TO REMEMBER THE DICTIONARY ORDER

You didn't think I would just leave you hanging with that, did you? In order to use a Korean dictionary, you will need to be able to remember the 한글 characters in their proper order. Let's have some fun and learn them now. You will probably need about 5 minutes or so to get this completely. Let's break them down into some smaller groups that will help us to remember them quickly and easily. Now, we just need a little sentence or two to set the order in our minds. Remember that silly is best when it comes to memory aides!

The characters always appear first with the vowel ㅏ after them and look like this:
가 나 다 라 마 바 사 아 자 차 카 타 파 하

Looks like a mouthful, doesn't it? It's only 14 characters though, and we can try to make our mnemonic sentence to remember the pattern.

Canada Llama? Bah!
Remember that ㄱ sometimes has a harder 'k' sound when in the initial position and ㄹ can be the 'L' sound, and the letter 'a' in phonetics always has the

'ah' sound. Now we have the first 6 in just a few seconds! 가 나 다, 라 마? 바!

Saw Ah Jar Pretend you're playing out a scene with Scarlet and Rhett, lay on the southern drawl, drop those final consonants, and you'll have added three more characters. Now we're more than halfway home. 사 아 자.

Chockataw Pa Ha! You might need to bend Choctaw to get this right, but it should be more than enough to holler out about your Indian father and add a little laugh to get the last five characters. 차 카 타 파 하!

Canada Llama? Bah!
Saw Ah Jar
Chockataw Pa Ha!

Run this little lyric through your head a few times in a sort of rhythmic chant, and don't forget to practice it out loud. Really loud two or three times would be great, if you're alone. Hey, if you're not, you can enjoy the idea that you've set all those other people around you to wondering just what in the world you're up to.

Dictionary Order: Note the 쌍 characters are listed here to help you, but are not usually considered to be part of the dictionary order as you learned in the previous mnemonic. Page numbers appear above the characters.

23	24	15	26	27	29	16
가	까	나	다	따	라	마
41	42	43	44	11	13	30
바	빠	사	싸	아	애	야
34	12	14	31	35	19	49
애	어	에	여	예	오	와
48	45	32	20	50	47	46
왜	외	요	우	워	웨	위
33	9	10	8	38	39	40
유	으	의	이	자	짜	차
25	28	18	17			
카	타	파	하			

Lesson Order: Here the characters are in the order in which they appear in each lesson.

(Lesson 1) 8	9	10	11	12	13	14
이	으	의	아	어	애	에
15	16	17	18	19	20	(Lesson 2) 23
나	마	하	파	오	우	가
24	25	26	27	28	29	30
까	카	다	따	타	라	야
31	32	33	34	35	(Lesson 3) 38	39
여	요	유	애	예	자	짜
40	41	42	43	44	45	46
차	바	빠	사	싸	외	위
47	48	49	50			
웨	왜	와	워			

TIPS FOR LEARNING A LANGUAGE

NOTE: While most of these tips seem geared specifically for learning Korean, in Korea, you'll find that they will apply to most language studies no matter where you are although access to some of the tools mentioned might not be as readily available.

Here are a few things to keep in mind when you are studying a second language. One thing to remember is that it is highly unlikely that anyone's life depends on your learning ability. My point? Language study should be fun and pressure free. Find fun ways to learn. If you enjoy singing, even if your friends don't enjoy yours, learn a Korean song. It's a great way to learn new vocabulary, sentence structures, and practice pronunciation. And, especially in Korea, visiting the 노래방 or 'singing room' is a favorite past time so it's handy to have a Korean song in your repertoire.

You can spend a lot of time waiting, no matter where you are. Make cards with vocabulary and sentences to study any time you aren't busy. The key here is variety. Shuffle the cards' order often. Keep the list on your cards short. Remember the principle that we remember best and easiest first parts and last parts.

Videos are also great learning tools. You can watch and rewind and they are plentiful. Continued exposure to the language will also help your mind to adjust to the cadence, rhythms, and structures of the language. Passive listening and active listening are both useful. Passive listening will subconsciously implant new vocabulary that can then be triggered when you are actually studying. It creates a sort of *deja vu*. Even watching movies in Korea in English can be helpful since they have Korean subtitles.

Video is the cheapest and most readily available, but if you have access to DVD, you have at your hands what might be one of the best language learning tools around. They provide multiple choices for subtitles and sound. You can listen to a movie in English with Korean subtitles. (This is also a great way to improve your reading speed.) You can also listen to a movie in Korean with English subtitles, or even Korean sound with Korean subtitles. I have not been able to find many Korean movies on DVD that have this option, but most animated films from the U.S. do have these options. Be careful though, not all of them do and the subtitles and translations can be slightly different from the actual script.

I have found in Korea a number of popular comic strips that have been published in books for students to learn English. The cartoons have a Korean translation next to each panel. I would read about 10 pages or so each day, blocking out the English, and reading only the Korean and looking at the pictures to try to get the context. Then I would go back for the words I didn't know, look them up in a dictionary, and write a short definition somewhere on the page, usually not next to the word. There are some mistakes in translation though so always be sure to check before you spend too much time memorizing the new vocabulary.

Don't trust your dictionary too much. When you want to know what a word means, dictionaries are great, but that doesn't always hold true when trying to learn new vocabulary. Just as English dictionaries are full of words native English speakers don't know or use commonly, Korean dictionaries are too. One thing I find helpful is to use my dictionary to find the word, for instance Korean to English, and then use my English to Korean dictionary to confirm the new word

I have found. Nothing beats asking a Korean native speaker though if the word you found is the most common one for the meaning you want.

Don't learn to say in Korean what you would say in English. What I mean is, direct translation can sometimes create funny, non-sensical, or even outright rude sentences in Korean. Find instead the phrase or expression that a Korean would use in a similar situation.

Practice, practice, practice. Study is great and of course we must, but it is more important to practice and use what we are learning. Reading books on swimming will get you drowned if you just read then jump in the pool. A good rule of thumb is about a 3:1 ratio of practice to study. This will serve you well as a beginner, but as your level progresses you'll spend even more time 'practicing' than studying. When you practice, practice at normal levels and use any appropriate actions to help re-enforce the vocabulary. We remember things we say, see, and do much more easily.

Conversation is an animal we can know. That means we can make a fairly good guess as to which direction a conversation is going to take. If we prepare in advance for possible responses, we can react more quickly and speak our new language more efficiently. Besides, using your new language is what it's all about. Koreans are usually very appreciative of even the smallest attempts at speaking Korean.

Memorize. Not just words. Memorize some standard responses or questions working your way up to some longer sentences that can be used in more than one situation. This allows you to speak with more confidence and can give you the time you need to think about your next response. Another fun thing to learn is an interesting expression. Expressions are as common in Korean as English and very useful for carrying along a conversation and making it more interesting and fun. (Fun, have I used that word enough?)

Don't just learn one way to say something. After you learn something, find at least one other way to say the same thing, changing a word here, or there. It's easier than it sounds since you'll only be adding a small piece of new information to information you already have stored in your long term memory.

Use links and associations. You'll be surprised at how you can gain new vocabulary by linking it to parts of words you already know. Also it's a good idea to learn pair words or opposites. For instance if you learn the word for 'good,' it's not so difficult to pair it with the word for 'bad.' An interesting thing about Korean in particular is that some words have meanings when the syllables are reversed. For instance 선생 means 'teacher.' Reverse the order to 생선 and you have the Korean word for 'fresh fish.' I'll leave it to you to form an association.

VOCABULARY

Shown in Korean alphabet order with page number in text.

-에 : to (something or place)(14)
가다 : to go(26)
가르치다 : to teach(40)
가위 : scissors(46)
강 : river(23)
계란 : egg(35)
공원 : park(50)
과일 : fruit(49)
과자 : snack(49)
괘씸하다 : to be insolent(48)
괜히 : in vain(48)
괴롭다 : troublesome(45)
꼬끼오 : cock-a-doodle-doo(24)
꿈 : dream(24)
나 : me(15)
나라 : country (29)
나의 : my(15, 21)
나이 : age(15)
낙타 : camel(28)
노인 : elderly person(19)
다 : all(26)
대답하다 : to answer(41)
뒈지다 : kick the bucket(47)

등등 : etc. etc.(26)
땀 : sweat(27)
때 : grime(27)
떠나다 : to leave(27)
라디오 : radio(29)
마음 : mind(16)
만 : 10,000(16)
매너 : manner(16)
매우 : very(21)
메모 : memo(21)
문 : door(20)
밥 : rice(41)
버터 : butter(41)
비싼 : expensive(44)
빨리 : fast, quickly(42)
뺨 : cheek(30)
뼈 : a bone (42)
뽀뽀 : light kiss(42)
사다 : to buy(43)
사랑 : love(43)
산 : mountain(43)
식권 : meal ticket(50)
싹 : (noun) sprout, bud(44)
쌍꺼풀 : double eyelid(44)
아 : oh(11)
아기: baby(23)
아까 : just before(24)

아이 : toddler(11)
애 : child(13)
야간 : night (as an adjective: night class)(30)
약 : medicine(30)
엄마 : mom(21)
여우 : fox(31)
여행 : travel(31)
역 : station(31)
예 : yes(35)
예약 : reservation(35)
오 : five(19)
오이 : cucumber(19)
오후 : afternoon(20)
왜 : why(48)
외국 : foreign country(45)
요금 : fare(32)
요요 : yoyo(32)
우아 : elegant(20)
우유 : milk(33)
원 : Korean currency(50)
웨딩 : wedding(47)
웬일 : what matter, what cause(47)
위대한 : great(46)
위험 : danger(46)
유리 : glass(33)
유아 : infant(33)
자 : ruler (for measuring)(38)

자다 : to sleep(38)
자동차 : automobile(40)
자유 : free (as in free time)(38)
짜다 : salty(39)
짜증 : annoyance(39)
찌르다 : to poke(39)
차 : tea(40)
카 : car(25)
코: nose(25)
키 : height(25)
타다 : to ride(28)
통 : container(28)
파마 : a permanent (for hair)(18)
펜 : pen(21)
피 : blood(18)
피아노 : piano(18)
하나 : one(17)
하마 : hippo(17)
학 : crane (the bird)(23)
학교 : school(32)
해 : sun(21)
화장품 : cosmetics(49)
회사 : company(45)
흠모 : admiration(21)
희망 : hope(21)
힘 : strength(17)

REVIEW VOCABULARY

LESSON ONE

이 으 의 아 어 애 에 나 마 하 파 오 우

하품 – yawn
미인 – beautiful person
애인 – lover, sweetheart
포함 – together, including
마음 – mind
잉어 – carp

앞에 – in front of
흥미 – interest
매미 – cicada
눈 – eye
남 – south
무우 – white radish

LESSON TWO

가 까 카 다 따 타 라 야 여 요 유 애 예

역 – station   약 – medicine
탈 – mask   깍다 – to cut down
켜다 – to light – a lamp   여유 – spare, extra
양 – sheep   여닫다 – open and shut
여탕 – ladies' public bath   육 – six
딱딱하다– To be headstrong; to be hard.

LESSON THREE

자 짜 차 바 빠 사 싸 와 외 위 웨 왜 워

쥐 - rat, mouse   방 - room

바위 - a rock, boulder   사 - four

사자 - lion   쇠 - iron

죄 - sin, crime   빵 - bread

사과 - apple   월 - month

ABOUT THE AUTHOR

Allen Williams grew up in southern Illinois then spent several years roaming around the western half of the U.S. After moving to Western Kentucky to finish college and later earning his M.A., he spent 6 years living, working, and studying in South Korea. He earned a Ph.D in 19th Century British and American poetry from Keimyung University in Taegu, South Korea. He has a first degree blackbelt in taekwondo, certified by the Kookiwon in Seoul. He is currently living and working in Nagoya, Japan with his wife and two sons. They share their time between Korea and Japan.